Jellyfish

This coloring book belongs to:

_____

_____

_____

Color Test

TEST YOUR COLOR SUPPLIES ON THIS PAGE

TO SEE HOW THEY REACT TO THE PAPER

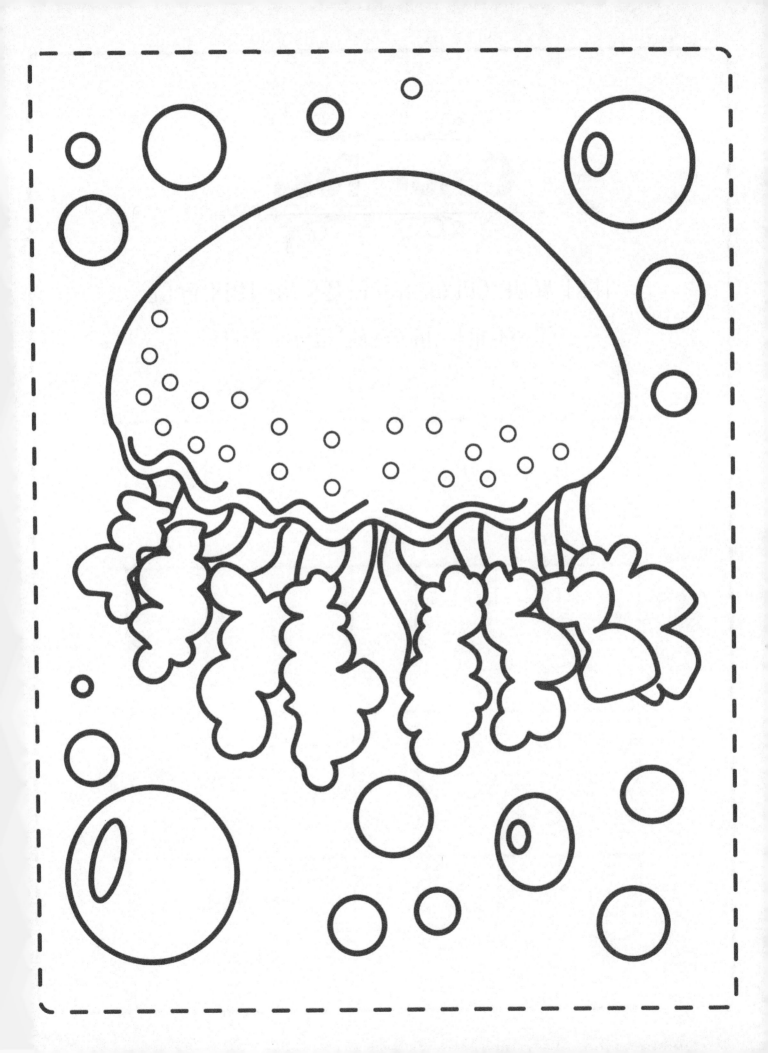

Color Test

TEST YOUR COLOR SUPPLIES ON THIS PAGE

TO SEE HOW THEY REACT TO THE PAPER

Color Test

TEST YOUR COLOR SUPPLIES ON THIS PAGE

TO SEE HOW THEY REACT TO THE PAPER

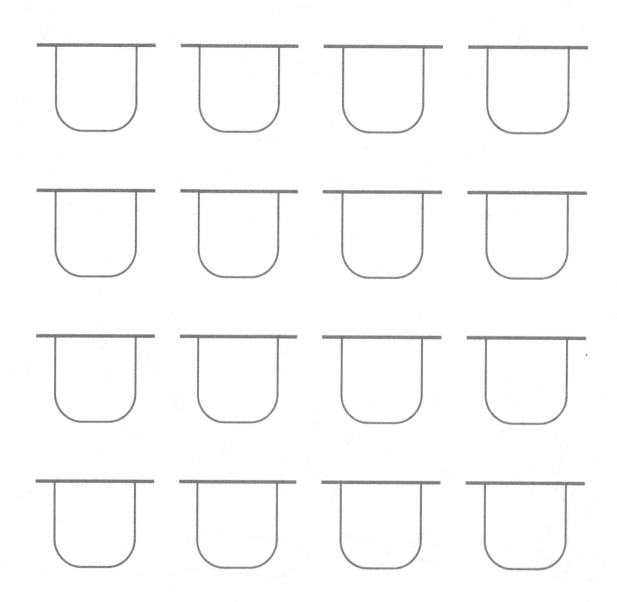

Color Test

TEST YOUR COLOR SUPPLIES ON THIS PAGE

TO SEE HOW THEY REACT TO THE PAPER

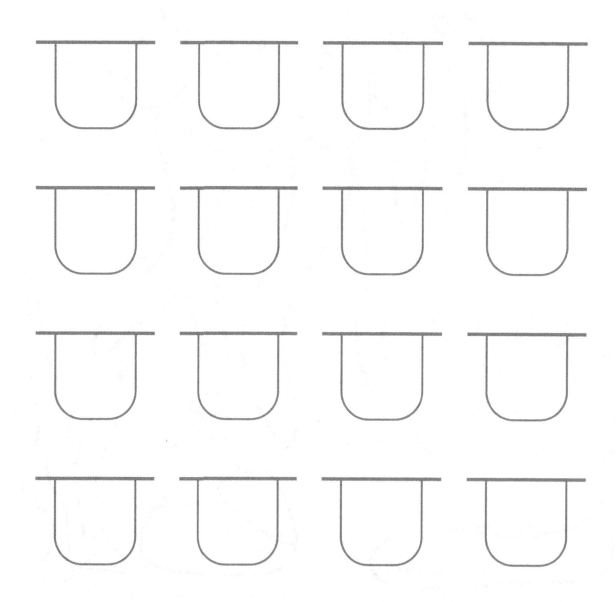

Color Test

TEST YOUR COLOR SUPPLIES ON THIS PAGE

TO SEE HOW THEY REACT TO THE PAPER

Color Test

TEST YOUR COLOR SUPPLIES ON THIS PAGE

TO SEE HOW THEY REACT TO THE PAPER

Color Test

TEST YOUR COLOR SUPPLIES ON THIS PAGE

TO SEE HOW THEY REACT TO THE PAPER

Color Test

TEST YOUR COLOR SUPPLIES ON THIS PAGE

TO SEE HOW THEY REACT TO THE PAPER

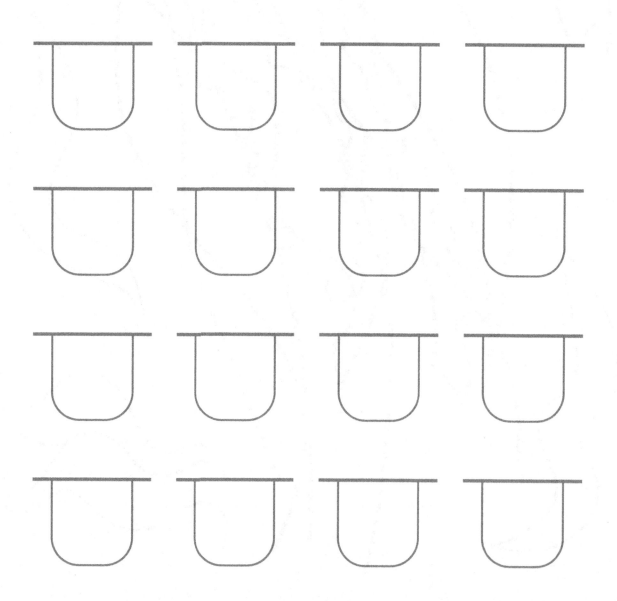

Color Test

TEST YOUR COLOR SUPPLIES ON THIS PAGE

TO SEE HOW THEY REACT TO THE PAPER

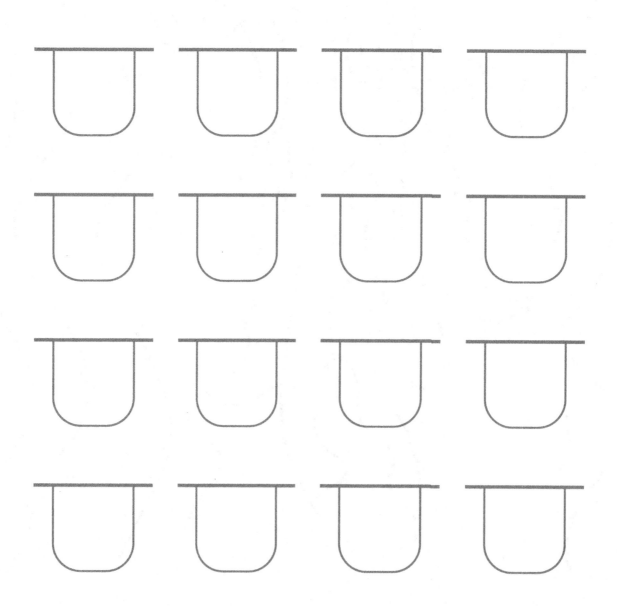

Color Test

TEST YOUR COLOR SUPPLIES ON THIS PAGE

TO SEE HOW THEY REACT TO THE PAPER

Color Test

TEST YOUR COLOR SUPPLIES ON THIS PAGE

TO SEE HOW THEY REACT TO THE PAPER

Color Test

TEST YOUR COLOR SUPPLIES ON THIS PAGE

TO SEE HOW THEY REACT TO THE PAPER

Color Test

TEST YOUR COLOR SUPPLIES ON THIS PAGE

TO SEE HOW THEY REACT TO THE PAPER

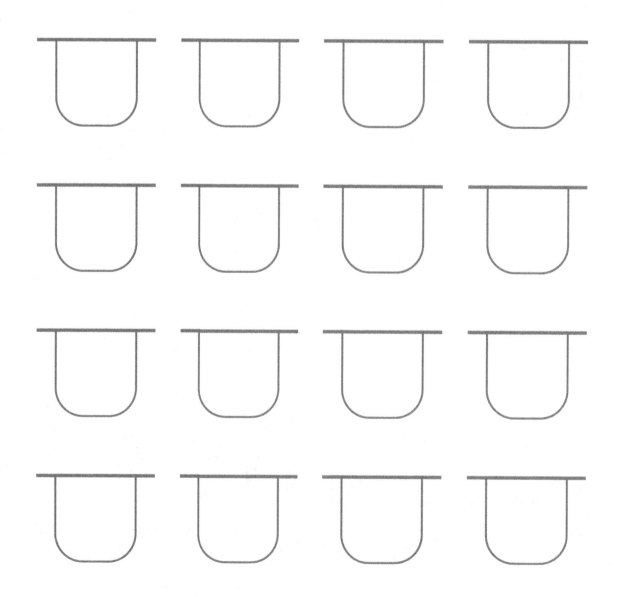

Color Test

TEST YOUR COLOR SUPPLIES ON THIS PAGE

TO SEE HOW THEY REACT TO THE PAPER

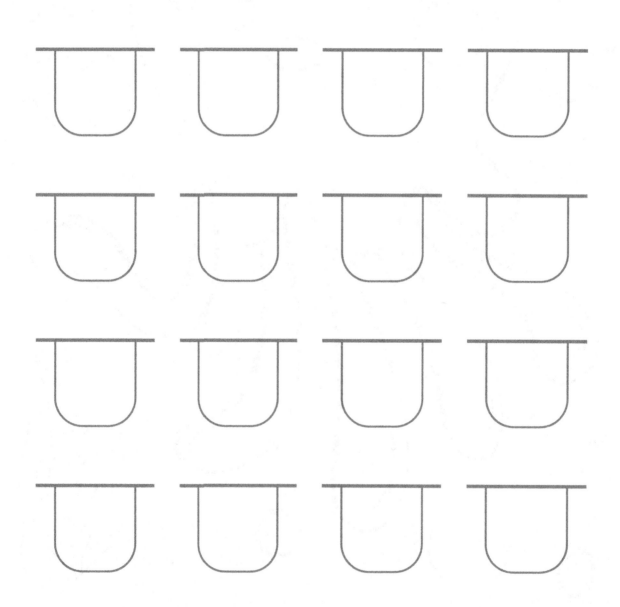

Color Test

TEST YOUR COLOR SUPPLIES ON THIS PAGE

TO SEE HOW THEY REACT TO THE PAPER

Color Test

TEST YOUR COLOR SUPPLIES ON THIS PAGE

TO SEE HOW THEY REACT TO THE PAPER

Color Test

TEST YOUR COLOR SUPPLIES ON THIS PAGE

TO SEE HOW THEY REACT TO THE PAPER

Color Test

TEST YOUR COLOR SUPPLIES ON THIS PAGE

TO SEE HOW THEY REACT TO THE PAPER

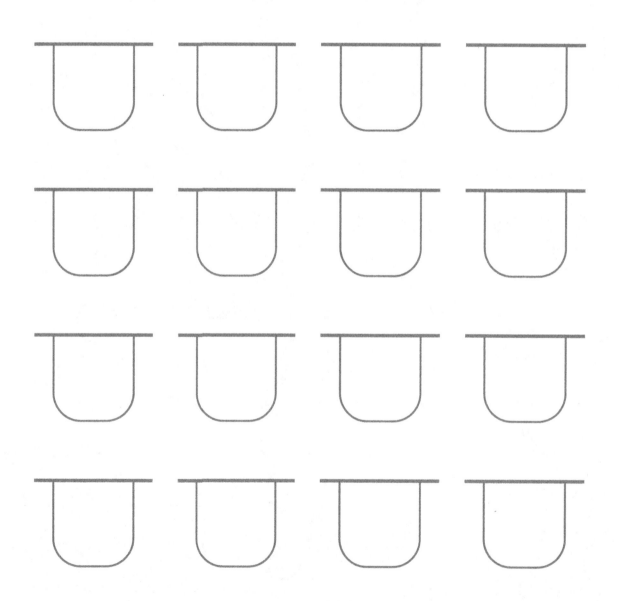

Color Test

TEST YOUR COLOR SUPPLIES ON THIS PAGE

TO SEE HOW THEY REACT TO THE PAPER

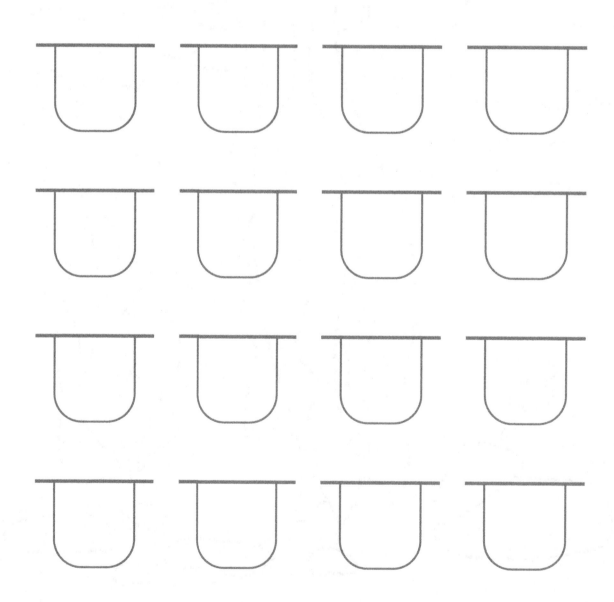

Color Test

TEST YOUR COLOR SUPPLIES ON THIS PAGE

TO SEE HOW THEY REACT TO THE PAPER

Color Test

TEST YOUR COLOR SUPPLIES ON THIS PAGE

TO SEE HOW THEY REACT TO THE PAPER

Color Test

TEST YOUR COLOR SUPPLIES ON THIS PAGE

TO SEE HOW THEY REACT TO THE PAPER

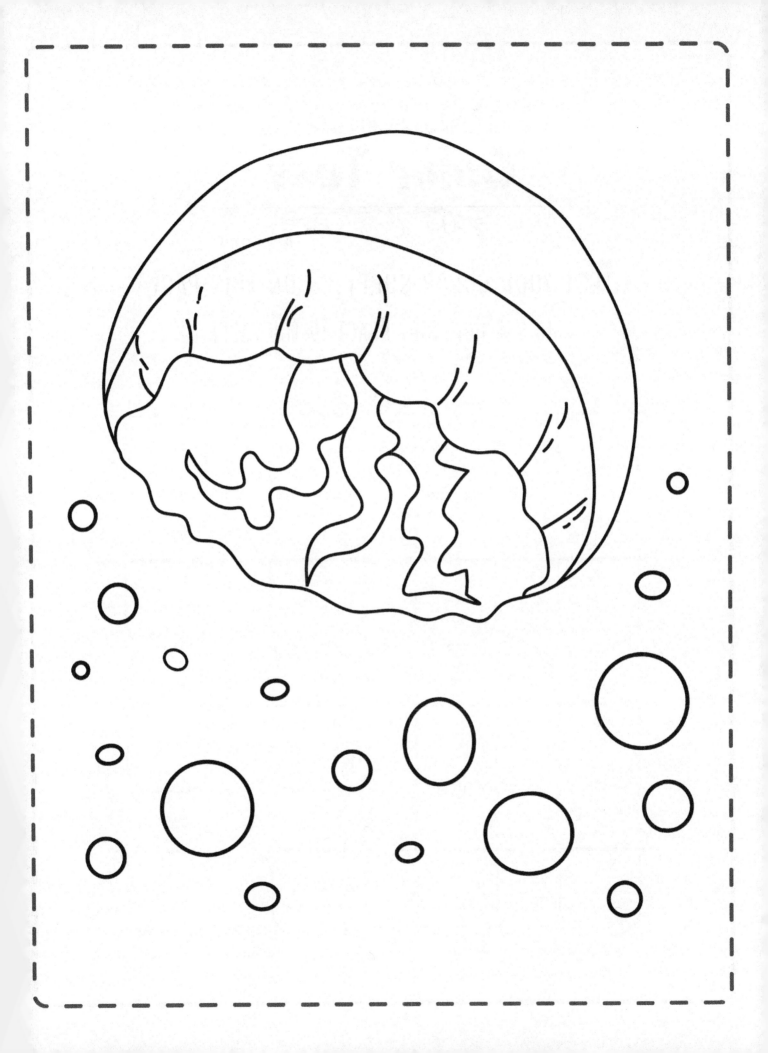

Color Test

TEST YOUR COLOR SUPPLIES ON THIS PAGE

TO SEE HOW THEY REACT TO THE PAPER

Color Test

TEST YOUR COLOR SUPPLIES ON THIS PAGE

TO SEE HOW THEY REACT TO THE PAPER

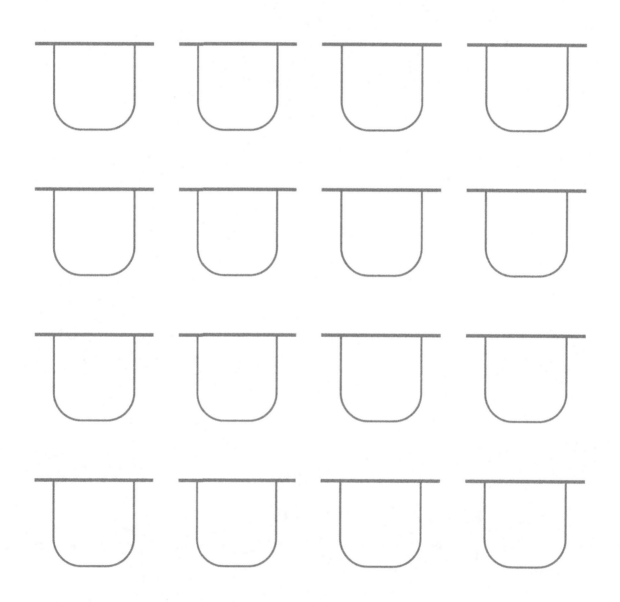

Color Test

TEST YOUR COLOR SUPPLIES ON THIS PAGE

TO SEE HOW THEY REACT TO THE PAPER

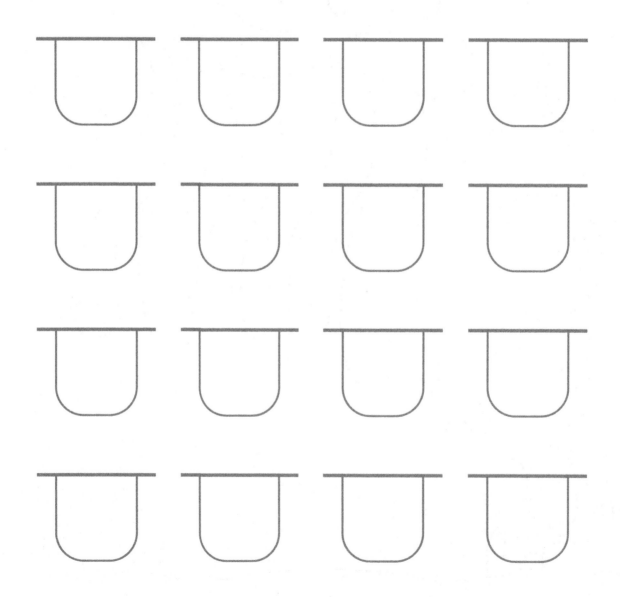

Color Test

TEST YOUR COLOR SUPPLIES ON THIS PAGE

TO SEE HOW THEY REACT TO THE PAPER

Color Test

TEST YOUR COLOR SUPPLIES ON THIS PAGE

TO SEE HOW THEY REACT TO THE PAPER

Color Test

TEST YOUR COLOR SUPPLIES ON THIS PAGE

TO SEE HOW THEY REACT TO THE PAPER

Color Test

TEST YOUR COLOR SUPPLIES ON THIS PAGE

TO SEE HOW THEY REACT TO THE PAPER

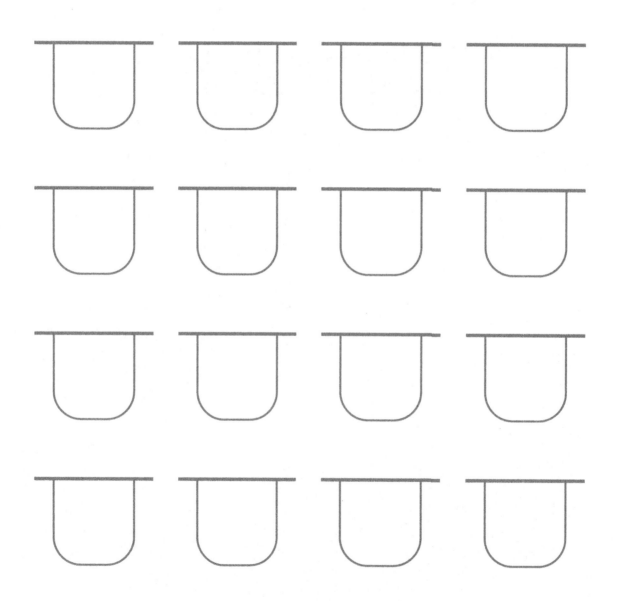

Color Test

TEST YOUR COLOR SUPPLIES ON THIS PAGE

TO SEE HOW THEY REACT TO THE PAPER

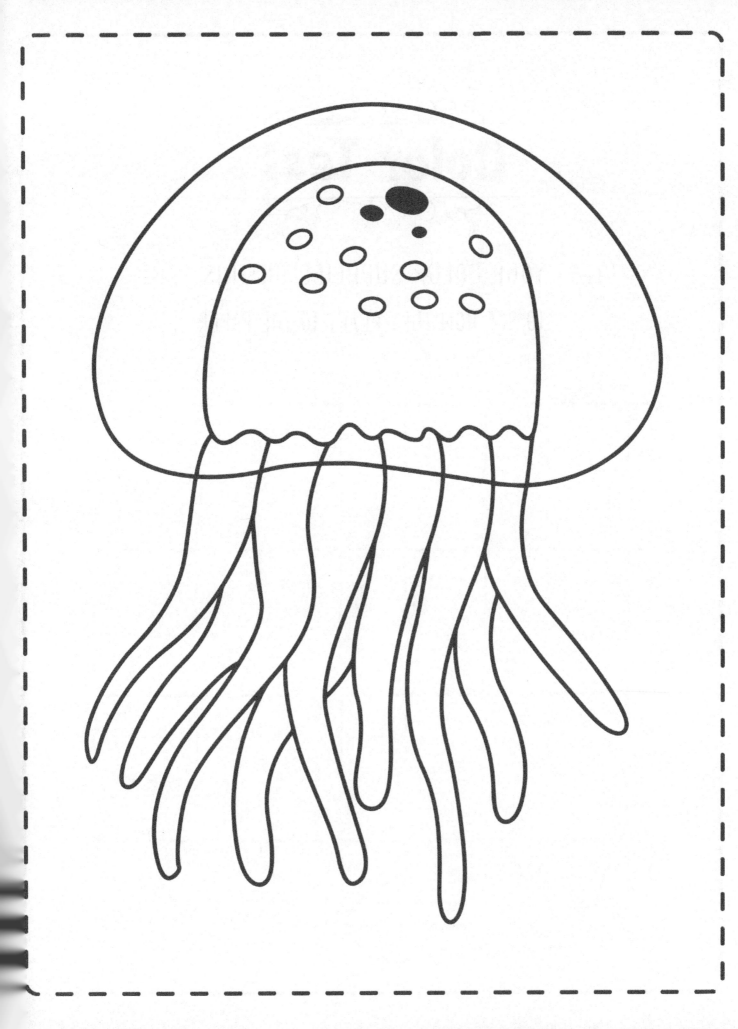

Color Test

TEST YOUR COLOR SUPPLIES ON THIS PAGE

TO SEE HOW THEY REACT TO THE PAPER

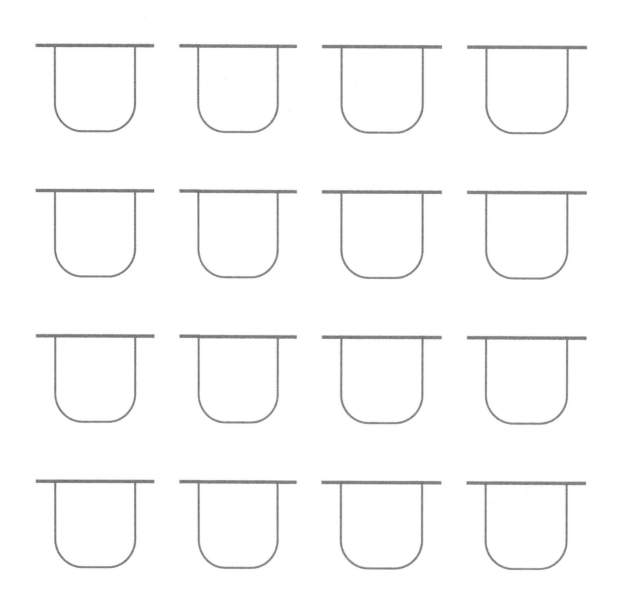

Color Test

TEST YOUR COLOR SUPPLIES ON THIS PAGE

TO SEE HOW THEY REACT TO THE PAPER

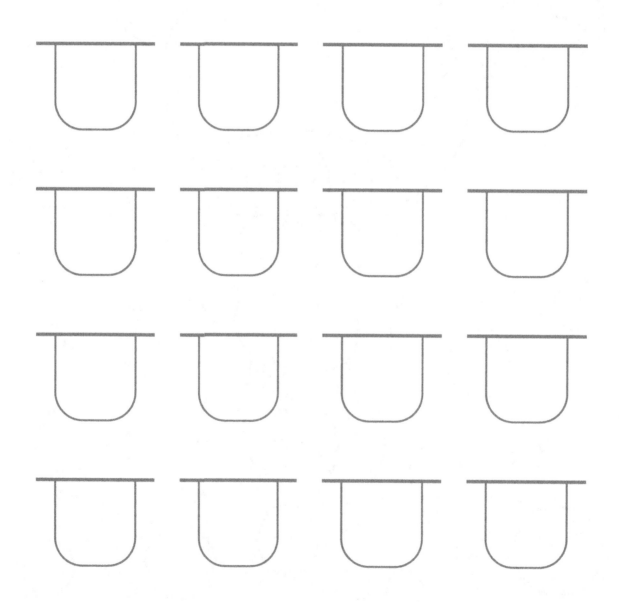

Color Test

TEST YOUR COLOR SUPPLIES ON THIS PAGE

TO SEE HOW THEY REACT TO THE PAPER

Color Test

TEST YOUR COLOR SUPPLIES ON THIS PAGE

TO SEE HOW THEY REACT TO THE PAPER

Color Test

TEST YOUR COLOR SUPPLIES ON THIS PAGE

TO SEE HOW THEY REACT TO THE PAPER

Color Test

TEST YOUR COLOR SUPPLIES ON THIS PAGE

TO SEE HOW THEY REACT TO THE PAPER

Color Test

TEST YOUR COLOR SUPPLIES ON THIS PAGE

TO SEE HOW THEY REACT TO THE PAPER

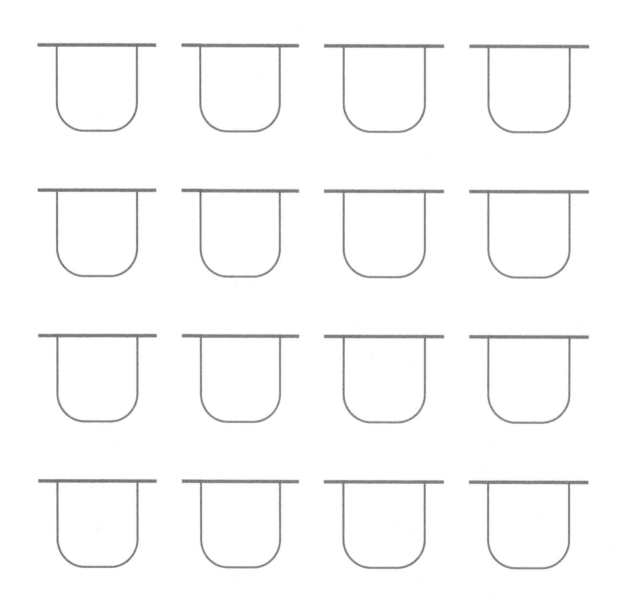

Color Test

TEST YOUR COLOR SUPPLIES ON THIS PAGE

TO SEE HOW THEY REACT TO THE PAPER

Color Test

TEST YOUR COLOR SUPPLIES ON THIS PAGE

TO SEE HOW THEY REACT TO THE PAPER

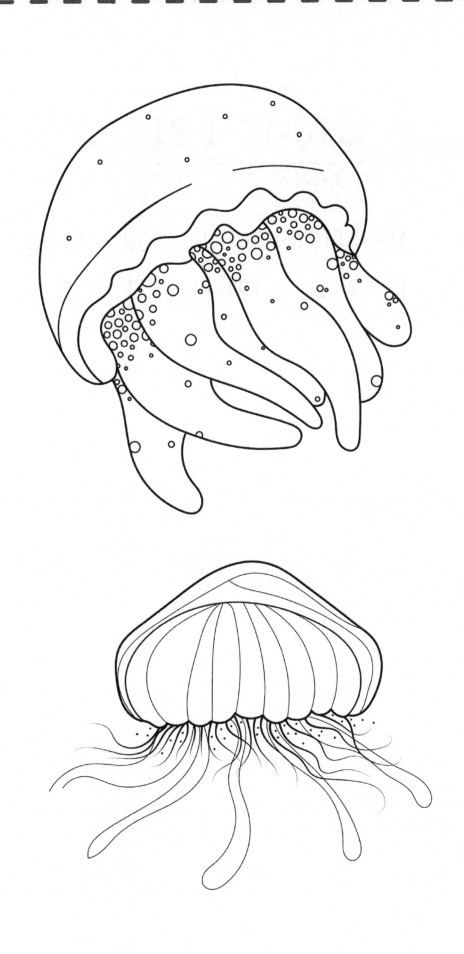

Color Test

TEST YOUR COLOR SUPPLIES ON THIS PAGE

TO SEE HOW THEY REACT TO THE PAPER

Color Test

TEST YOUR COLOR SUPPLIES ON THIS PAGE

TO SEE HOW THEY REACT TO THE PAPER

Color Test

TEST YOUR COLOR SUPPLIES ON THIS PAGE

TO SEE HOW THEY REACT TO THE PAPER

Color Test

TEST YOUR COLOR SUPPLIES ON THIS PAGE

TO SEE HOW THEY REACT TO THE PAPER

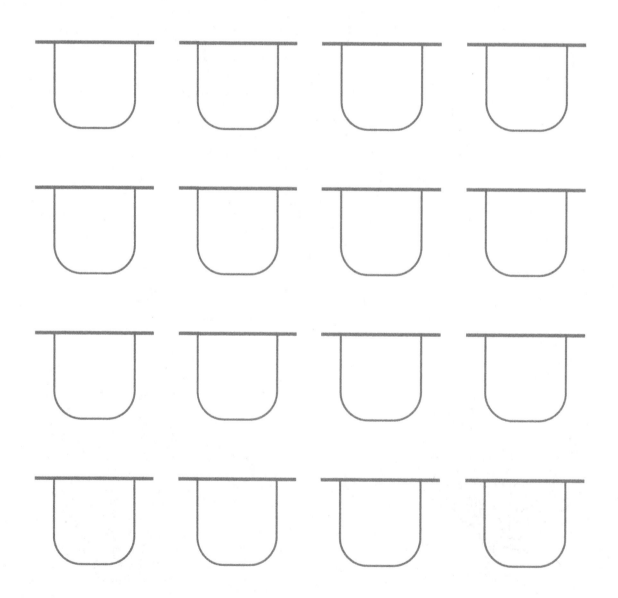

Made in the USA
Columbia, SC
20 September 2024